Enchantment

First published in Great Britain in 1996 by
BROCKHAMPTON PRESS
20 Bloomsbury Street, London WC1B 3QA
a member of the Hodder Headline Group

This series of little gift books was made by Frances Banfield, Andrea P.A. Belloli, Polly Boyd,
Kate Brown, Stefano Carantino, Laurel Clark, Penny Clarke, Clive Collins, Jack Cooper, Melanie Cumming,
Nick Diggory, John Dunne, Deborah Gill, David Goodman, Paul Gregory, Douglas Hall, Lucinda Hawksley,
Maureen Hill, Dennis Hovell, Dicky Howett, Nick Hutchison, Douglas Ingram, Helen Johnson, C.M. Lee,
Simon London, Irene Lyford, John Maxwell, Patrick McCreeth, Morse Modaberi, Tara Neill, Sonya Newland,
Anne Newman, Grant Oliver, Ian Powling, Terry Price, Michelle Rogers, Mike Seabrook,
Nigel Soper, Karen Sullivan and Nick Wells.

Compilation and selection copyright © 1996 Brockhampton Press.
Illustrations Copyright © 1996 Jean and Ron Henry

ISBN 1 86019 4737
A copy of the CIP data is available from the British Library upon request.

Produced for Brockhampton Press by Flame Tree Publishing,
a part of The Foundry Creative Media Company Limited,
The Long House, Antrobus Road, Chiswick W4 5HY.

Printed and bound in Italy by L.E.G.O. Spa.

CELEBRATION

Enchantment

Selected by Karen Sullivan

Illustrations by Jean and Ron Henry

BROCKHAMPTON PRESS

Black magic operates most effectively in preconscious, marginal areas. Casual curses are the most effective.

William Burroughs

The children did not tell their father and mother about the happenings in the Enchanted Wood, for they were so afraid that they might be forbidden to go there. But when they were alone they talked about nothing else.

Enid Blyton, *The Enchanted Wood*

We are such stuff
As dreams are made on; and our little life
Is rounded with a sleep.

William Shakespeare, *The Tempest*

The hills are shadows, and they flow
From form to form, and nothing stands;
They melt like mist, the solid lands,
Like clouds they shape themselves and go.

Alfred, Lord Tennyson, *'In Memoriam'*

We are the music-makers,
And we are the dreamers of dreams,
Wandering by lone sea-breakers,
And sitting by desolate streams:
World-losers and world-forsakers,
On whom the pale moon gleams:
Yet we are the movers and shakers
Of the world for ever, it seems.

Arthur O'Shaughnessy, *'The Music Makers'*

Imagination is the eye of the soul.

Joseph Joubert

The good Bishop Vincent of Beauvais testified that a concoction of heliotrope, drunk with the invocation of powerful enough spirits, had the power to give invisibility at will.

From every leaf and petal dropped bright water. It gathered slowly at each point, but the points were so many that there was a constant musical plashing of diamond rain upon the still surface of the lake. As they went on, the moon rose and threw a pale mist of light over the whole, and the diamond drops turned to half-liquid pearls, and round every tree-top was a halo of moonlight, and the water went to sleep, and the flowers began to dream.

George Macdonald, *Cross Purposes*

Indubitably, Magick is one of the subtlest and most difficult of the sciences and arts. There is more opportunity for errors of comprehension, judgement and practice than in any other branch of physics.

Aleister Crowley

Nobody has any conscience about adding to the improbabilities of a marvelous tale.

Nathaniel Hawthorne

My imagination makes me human and makes me a fool; it gives me all the world and exiles me from it.

Ursula K. Le Guin

Can a magician a fortune divine
Without lily, germander, and sops-in-wine?

'Rhyme of Robin Goodfellow'

The hunchèd camels of the night

Trouble the bright
And silver waters of the moon.
The Maiden of the Morn will soon
Through Heaven stray and sing,
Star gathering.

Francis Thompson, *'Arab Love Song'*

 11

As a world that has no well,
Darkly bright in forest dell;
As a world without the gleam
Of the downward-going stream…

George Macdonald, *'The Light Princess'*

Shadows, Shadows, Shadows all!
Shadow birth and funeral!
Shadow moons gleam overhead:
Over shadow-graves we tread.

George Macdonald, *'The Shadows'*

There was no answer and
Edmund noticed that his
own voice had a curious
sound – not the sound you
expect in a cupboard, but
a kind of open-air sound.
He also noticed that he
was unexpectedly cold;
and then he saw a light.

C. S. Lewis, *The Lion, the Witch
and the Wardrobe*

Ye elves of hills, brooks, standing lakes, and groves,
And ye that on the sands with printless foot
Do chase the ebbing Neptune, and do fly him
When he comes back; you demi-puppets that
By moonshine do the green, sour ringlets make
Whereof the ewe not bites; and you whose pastime
Is to make the midnight mushrumps, that rejoice
To hear the solemn curfew, by whose aid –
Weak masters though ye be – I have bedimmed
The noontide sun, called forth the mutinous winds,
And 'twixt the green sea and the azured vault
Set roaring war.

William Shakespeare, *The Tempest*

In fairy-tales, witches always wear silly black hats and black cloaks, and they ride on broomsticks.

But this is not a fairy-tale. This is about REAL WITCHES. The most important thing you should know about real witches is this. Listen very carefully. Never forget what is coming next.

REAL WITCHES dress in ordinary clothes and look very much like ordinary women. They live in ordinary houses and they work in ORDINARY JOBS.

That is why they are so hard to catch.

Roald Dahl, *The Witches*

A belief is like a guillotine, just as heavy, just as light.

Franz Kafka

I will make you brooches and toys for your delight
Of bird-song at morning and star-shine at night.

Robert Louis Stevenson, *'Romance'*

You spotted snakes, with double tongue,
Thorny hedgehogs, be not seen;
Newts and blind-worms do no wrong,
Come not near our fairy queen.

William Shakespeare, *A Midsummer-Night's Dream*

A drowsy numbness pains my senses
As if of hemlock I had drunk.

John Keats, *'Ode to a Nightingale'*

In Xanadu did Kubla Khan
A stately pleasure-dome decree:
Where Alph, the sacred river, ran
Through caverns measureless to man
Down to a sunless sea.

Samuel Taylor Coleridge, *'Kubla Khan'*

In an ancient meadow,
By the twilight's glow,
You might see a fairy,
Just where the bluebells grow.
And you may try and catch one,
If you can take your time.
Hold it gently on a twig,
Until the bluebells chime.
Alas you cannot keep one,
Though you wish you could,
For when you hear the bluebell's chime,
There'll be nothing where they stood.

Jean Henry, *Twilight*

A little weeping fairy found
A patch of sunshine on the ground.
She knew it was the very thing,
To mend a hole torn in her wing.
She dried her eyes, picked up the patch,
And saw it would exactly match.
So sitting beneath a tree they say,
She sewed it on and flew away.
The tree then shook its leaves and made,
A shadow where the patch had played,
So that the sun should never guess
That now he owns just one patch less.

Anonymous, *The Stolen Patch*

The imagination is the spur of delights…
all depends upon it, it is the mainspring
of everything; now, is it not by means of
the imagination one knows joy? Is it not
of the imagination that the sharpest
pleasures arise?

Marquis de Sade

The moon was a ghostly galleon tossed
upon cloudy seas.

Alfred Noyes, *The Highwayman*

If a little dreaming is dangerous, the cure for it is not to dream less but to dream more, to dream all the time.

Marcel Proust

Dream is not a revelation. If a dream affords the dreamer some light on himself, it is not the person with closed eyes who makes the discovery but the person with open eyes lucid enough to fit thoughts together. Dream – a scintillating mirage surrounded by shadows – is essentially poetry.

Michel Leiris

Full fathom five thy father lies,
Of his bones are coral made;
Those are pearls that were his eyes,
Nothing of him that doth fade,
But doth suffer a sea-change
Into something rich and strange.

William Shakespeare, *The Tempest*

Up and down, up and down;
I will lead them up and down:
I am fear'd in field and town;
Goblin, lead them up and down.

William Shakespeare, *A Midsummer-Night's Dream*

To make a prairie it takes a clover and one bee,
One clover, and a bee,
And revery.
The revery alone will do,
If bees are few.

Emily Dickinson

Fetch me that flower;
The herb I show'd thee once:
The juice of it on sleeping eyelids laid
Will make a man or woman madly dote
Upon the next live creature that it sees.

William Shakespeare, *A Midsummer-Night's Dream*

Heard melodies are sweet, but those unheard
Are sweeter.

John Keats, *'Ode on a Grecian Urn'*

What thou seest when thou dost wake,
Do it for thy true love take;
Love and languish for his sake:
Be it ounce, or cat, or bear,
Pard, or boar with bristled hair,
In thy eye that shall appear,
When thou wak'st, it is thy dear.
Wake when some vile thing is near.

William Shakespeare, *A Midsummer-Night's Dream*

One Ring to rule them all, One Ring to find them,
One Ring to bring them all and in the darkness bind them
Three Rings for the Elven-kings under the sky,
Seven for the Dwarf-lords in their halls of stone,
Nine for Mortal Men doomed to die,
One for the Dark Lord on his dark throne
In the Land of Mordor where the Shadows lie.
One Ring to rule them all, One Ring to find them,
One Ring to bring them all and in the darkness bind them
In the Land of Mordor where the Shadows lie.

J. R. R. Tolkien, *The Lord of the Rings*

My imagination is a monastery and I am its monk.

John Keats

How fading are the joys we dote upon!
Like apparitions seen and gone.
But those which soonest take their flight
Are the most exquisite and strong –
Like angels' visits, short and bright;
Mortality's too weak to bear them long.

John Norris, *'The Parting'*

Safe upon the solid rock the ugly houses stand:
Come and see my shining palace built upon the sand!

Edna St Vincent Millay, *'Second Fig'*

We say God and the imagination are one...
How high the highest candle lights the dark.

Wallace Stevens

Where there is no imagination there is no horror.

Sir Arthur Conan Doyle

Heaven's ebon vault,
Studded with stars unutterably bright,
Through which the moon's unclouded
grandeur rolls,
Seems like a canopy which love has spread
To curtain her sleeping world.

Percy Bysshe Shelley, *'Queen Mab'*

Silently, one by one, in the infinite meadows of heaven,
Blossomed the lovely stars, the forget-me-nots of the angels.

Henry Wadsworth Longfellow, *'Evangeline'*

For more than two hundred years, the Owens women have been blamed for everything that has gone wrong in town. If a damp spring arrived, if cows in the pasture gave milk that was runny with blood, if a colt died of colic or a baby was born with a red birthmark stamped onto his cheek, everyone believed that fate must have been twisted, at least a little, by those women over on Magnolia Street.

Alice Hoffman, *Practical Magic*

The first law of story-telling... Every man is bound to leave a story better than he found it.

Mrs Humphrey Ward

Taste the quivering
shimmering
dew
Catch it as it gleams
for a moment
The wing of a faery
in flight
Enchanted air
And gone.

Kitty Browne

The dream of reason produces monsters. Imagination deserted by reason creates impossible, useless thoughts. United with reason, imagination is the mother of all art and the source of all its beauty.

Francisco José de Goya y Lucientes

But in the heart of the Border country, where the wind howls with cold, bad is almost always balanced by good, and so it was then when from that night onwards, Parcie's mother never again had to say to him, 'Parcie, it's time for your bed,' for at the first sudden movement of the shadows, when the fire began to sink down into red-black embers, he was sound asleep in his tiny box-bed, deep in the sleep of the golden slumberdust.

K. E. Sullivan, *The Brownie*

Do you see the lantern seller?
Oh! he's such a happy feller,
Making lanterns just so many,
Selling them for half a penny!

Ron Henry, *'The Lantern Seller'*

Go and catch a falling star,
Get with child a mandrake root,
Tell me where all past years are,
Or who cleft the Devil's foot;
Teach me to hear mermaids singing.

John Donne, *'Song'*

Through a little hole in the wall the children had crept in, and they were sitting in the branches of the trees. In every tree that he could see there was a little child. And the trees were so glad to have the children back again that they had covered themselves with blossoms, and were waving their arms gently above the children's heads. The birds were flying about and twittering with delight, and the flowers were looking up through the green grass and laughing.

Oscar Wilde, *The Selfish Giant*

Listen, little Elia: draw your chair up close to the edge of the precipice and I'll tell you a story.

F. Scott Fitzgerald

If so be a Toad be laid
In a sheep's-skin newly flaid,
And that ty'd to man, 'twil sever
Him and his affections ever.

Robert Herrick, *'A Charme, or an Allay for Love'*

And he began the spell for use at nights
In all four corners of the room and out
Across the threshold too and round about:
Jesu Christ and Benedict sainted
Bless this house from creatures tainted,
Drive away night-hags, white Pater-noster,
Where did you go, St Peter's soster?

Geoffrey Chaucer, *The Canterbury Tales*

50

A good story cannot be devised; it has to be distilled.

Raymond Chandler

Bid me discourse, I will enchant thine ear,
Or like a fairy trip upon the green,
Or, like a nymph, with long dishevell'd hair,
Dance on the sands, and yet no footing seen.

William Shakespeare, *'Venus and Adonis'*

Science has explained nothing; the more we know the more fantastic the world becomes and the profounder the surrounding darkness.

Aldous Huxley

Educating a son I should allow him no fairy tales and only a very few novels. This is to prevent him from having 1. the sense of romantic solitude (if he is worth anything he will develop a proper and useful solitude) which identification with the hero gives. 2. cant ideas of right and wrong, absurd systems of honor and morality which never never will he be able completely to get rid of. 3. the attainment of 'ideals' of a priori desires, of a priori emotions. He should amuse himself with fact only: he will then not learn that if the weak younger son do or do not the magical honorable thing he will win the princess with hair like flax.

Lionel Trilling

'Enjoy yourself,' said the fairy godmother, 'but remember, you must be home by midnight. For at the stroke of twelve, your coach will become a pumpkin, your footmen will become lizards, and your dress will change back into striped cotton.' Without waiting to be thanked, the lady vanished. Cinderella jumped joyfully into the coach and set off for the ball.

Cinderella

Imagination is the voice of daring. If there is anything God-like about God it is that He dared to imagine everything.

Henry Miller

An evil spirit, your beauty, haunts me still,
Wherewith, alas! I have been long possessed.

Michael Drayton, *Sonnets to Ideas*

Thrice toss these oaken ashes in the air;
Thrice sit thou mute in this enchanted chair;
Then thrice three times tie up this true love's knot,
And murmur soft: 'She will or she will not.'

Thomas Campion, *'Song for the Lute'*

Come away, O human child!
To the waters and the wild
With a faery, hand in hand...

W. B. Yeats, *'The Stolen Child'*

Like some bold seer in a trance,
Seeing all his own mischance –
With a glassy countenance
Did she look to Camelot.

Alfred, Lord Tennyson, *'The Lady of Shallot'*

I saw pale kings and princes too,
Pale warriors, death-pale were they all;
They cried – 'La Belle Dame Sans Merci
Hath thee in thrall.'

John Keats, *'La Belle Dame Sans Merci'*

I arise from dreams of thee
In the first sweet sleep of night.
When the winds are breathing low,
And the stars are shining bright.

Percy Bysshe Shelley, *'The Indian Serenade'*

On the ground
Sleep sound:
I'll apply
To your eye,
Gentle lover, remedy.

William Shakespeare, *A Midsummer-Night's Dream*

When at home alone I sit
And am very tired of it,
I have just to shut my eyes
To go sailing through the skies –
To go sailing far away
To the pleasant Land of Play;
To the fairy land afar
Where the Little People are…

Robert Louis Stevenson, *'The Little Land'*

Lost, yesterday, somewhere between Sunrise and Sunset, two golden hours, each set with sixty diamond minutes. No reward is offered, for they are gone forever.

Horace Mann, *Lost, Two Golden Hours*

A witch is one who worketh by the Devil or by some curious art either healing or revealing things secret, or foretelling things to come which the Devil hath devised to ensnare men's souls withal unto damnation. The conjurer, the enchanter, the sorcerer, the diviner, and whatever other sort there is encompassed within this circle.

George Gifford, English clergyman, 16th-century

Dear Beauty, I was doomed by a wicked fairy to wear the mask of a monster and to live a life of sorrow and loneliness until someone should love me despite my terrible looks. Only when I could find it inside myself to love, and to be loved in return, could I be freed. Your compassion has broken the spell.

Beauty and the Beast

We are lonesome animals. We spend all our life trying to be less lonesome. One of our ancient methods is to tell a story begging the listener to say – and to feel – 'Yes, that's the way it is, or at least that's the way I feel it. You're not as alone as you thought.'

John Steinbeck

Is it not strange, that an infant should be heir of the whole world, and see those mysteries which the books of the learned never unfold?

Thomas Traherne

There is something haunting in the light of the moon; it has all the dispassionateness of a disembodied soul, and something of its inconceivable mystery.

Joseph Conrad

A woman clothed with the sun, and the moon under her feet, and upon her head a crown of twelve stars.

Revelation, XII:1

And one knows it sometimes when one stands by oneself in a wood at sunset and the mysterious deep gold stillness slanting through and under the branches seems to be saying slowly again and again something one cannot quite hear, however much one tries…

Frances Hodgson Burnett, *The Secret Garden*

At the same time that we are earnest to explore and learn all things, we require that all things be mysterious and unexplorable, that land and sea be infinitely wild, unsurveyed and unfathomed by us because unfathomable.

Henry David Thoreau

What stately vision mocks my waking sense?
Hence, dear delusion, sweet enchantment, hence!

James Smith, *An Address without a Phoenix*

So flashed and fell the brand Excalibur:
But ere he dipt the surface, rose an arm
Clothed in white samite, mystic, wonderful,
And caught him by the hilt and brandished him
Three times, and drew him in under the mere.

Alfred, Lord Tennyson, *The Passing of Arthur*

Be not afeard. The isle is full of noises,
Sounds and sweet airs, that give delight and hurt not.

William Shakespeare, *The Tempest*

They also say, if earth or stone,
From verdant Erin's hallowed land,
Were on this magic island thrown,
For ever fixed, it then would stand,
But, when for this, some little boat
In silence ventures from the shore –
The mermaid sinks – hushed is the note,
The fairy isle is seen no more!

Anonymous, *The Enchanted Island*

To pass the oak in vain he tried;
His steed refused to stir,
Though furious 'gainst his panting side
Was struck the bloody spur.
The moon, by driving clouds o'ercast,
Witheld its fitful gleam;
And louder than the tempest blast
Was heard the Banshee's scream.

Anonymous, *Earl Desmond and the Banshee*

Over the hill and just past that little bend in the road, you'll find it. There. A house – a little older than the others, but not really different in any way. It's set back from the road, this house, and it has lovely iron fences which guard its secrets.

This is a special house. As you walk down the drive towards it, you can feel it. There. A funny feeling. And if you close your eyes and listen very hard, you'll hear something. Walk through the house and the feeling becomes stronger. Walk slowly, right through the house and out the back.

There. The garden. Can you feel it? It's magic. And that's where our story begins.

Kitty Browne, *The Magic Garden*

But those rare souls whose spirit gets magically into the hearts of men, leave behind them something more real and warmly personal than bodily presence, an ineffable and eternal thing. It is everlasting life touching us as something more than a vague, recondite concept. The sound of a great name dies like an echo; the splendor of fame fades into nothing; but the grace of a fine spirit pervades the places through which it has passed, like the haunting loveliness of mignonette.

James Thurber

In the tale, in the telling, we are all one blood. Take the tale in your teeth, then, and bite till the blood runs, hoping it's not poison; and we will all come to the end together, and even to the beginning: living, as we do, in the middle.

Ursula K. Le Guin

That blessed mood
In which the burthen of the mystery,
In which the heavy and the weary weight
Of all this unintelligible world
Is lightened.

William Wordsworth

I did send,
After the last enchantment you did here,
A ring in chase of you.

William Shakespeare, *Twelfth Night*

So she sat on, with closed eyes, and half believed herself in Wonderland, though she knew she had but to open them again, and all would change to dull reality – the grass would be only rustling in the wind, and the pool rippling to the waving of the reeds – the rattling teacups would change to tinkling sheep-bells, and the Queen's shrill cries to the voice of the shepherd boy – and the sneeze of the baby, the shriek of the Gryphon, and all the other queer noises, would change (she knew) to the confused clamour of the busy farmyard – while the lowing of the cattle in the distance would take the place of the Mock Turtle's heavy sobs. Lastly, she pictured to herself how this same little sister of hers would, in the aftertime, be herself a grown woman; and how she would keep, through all her riper years, the simple and loving heart of her childhood; and how she would gather about her other little children, and make their eyes bright and eager with many a strange tale, perhaps even with the dream of Wonderland of long ago…

Lewis Carroll, *Alice's Adventures in Wonderland*

The feet of the dead Witch had disappeared entirely and nothing was left but the silver shoes. 'She was so old,' explained the Witch of the North, 'that she dried up quickly in the sun. That is the end of her. But the silver shoes are yours, and you shall have to wear them…'

L. Frank Baum, *The Wonderful Wizard of Oz*

On tiptoe he passed from one beautiful room to another, some with walls of looking-glass, some with walls of mother-of-pearl, some with walls of ivory. At last, in the very centre of the palace, he came to the room where the Princess lay in her enchanted sleep. At either end of her golden bed sat a lady-in-waiting, as fast asleep as she. Across the threshold her page slept, with his lute in his hand. At her feet slumbered a fluffy white dog, and in the silver cage by her pillow three little birds with brightly coloured plumes were dreaming, each with his head tucked under his wing.

Sleeping Beauty

There she weaves by night and day
A magic web with colours gay.
She has heard a whisper say,
A curse is on her if she stay
To look down to Camelot.

Alfred, Lord Tennyson, *'The Lady of Shalott'*

From the very fountain of enchantment there arises a taste of
bitterness to spread anguish amongst the flowers.

Lucretius

Notes on Illustrations

All illustrations courtesy of Ron and Jean Henry.

Page 1 *The Stolen Patch* by Jean and Ron Henry; **Page 3** *Down in the Woods* by Jean and Ron Henry; **Page 4** *Summer Evening;* **Page 7** *Enchanted* by Jean Henry; **Page 9** *Mermaids* by Jean Henry; **Page 10** *The Fairy Wedding* by Jean and Ron Henry; **Page 12** *Moon Maiden;* **Page 14** *Davy Jones' Locker* by Ron Henry; **Page 17** *Sweet Blossom* by Jean Henry; **Page 18** *Spellbound* by Jean Henry; **Page 20** *The Fairy Story* by Jean Henry; **Page 25** *The Snowstorm* by Ron Henry; **Page 26** *The First Meeting* by Jean and Ron Henry; **Page 29** *Summer Evening;* **Page 30** *Spellbound* by Jean Henry; **Page 33** *Fairy Doll* by Jean Henry; **Page 37** *Rainbow Glen* by Jean and Ron Henry; **Page 39** *Twilight* by Jean and Ron Henry; **Page 41** *Magic Pool* by Jean and Ron Henry; **Page 42** *Swan Ride* by Jean Henry; **Page 45** *Bottom of the Garden* by Jean and Ron Henry; **Page 47** *The Lantern Seller* by Ron Henry; **Page 49** *Neptune's Daughters* by Jean and Ron Henry; **Page 50** *The Fairy Wedding* by Jean and Ron Henry; **Page 54** *Davy Jones' Locker* by Ron Henry; **Page 57** *The First Meeting* by Jean and Ron Henry; **Page 58** *Bottom of the Garden* by Jean and Ron Henry; **Page 61** *Spellbound* by Jean Henry; **Page 65** *Rainbow Glen* by Jean and Ron Henry; **Page 67** *Sweet Blossom* by Jean Henry; **Page 68** *Magic Pool* by Jean and Ron Henry; **Page 70** *Rainbow Glen* by Jean and Ron Henry; **Page 72** *The Fairy Story* by Jean Henry; **Page 77** *Bottom of the Garden* by Jean and Ron Henry; **Page 78** *Magic Pool* by Jean and Ron Henry; **Page 81** *Swan Ride* by Jean Henry; **Page 82** *Neptune's Daughters* by Jean and Ron Henry.

Acknowledgements: The Publishers wish to thank everyone who gave permission to reproduce the quotes in this book. Every effort has been made to contact the copyright holders, but in the event that an oversight has occurred, the publishers would be delighted to rectify any omissions in future editions of this book. Roald Dahl, reprinted courtesy of George Allen & Unwin Publishers Ltd © 1970 Roald Dahl; Kitty Browne reproduced courtesy of The Foundry Creative Media Company; Enid Blyton, published by Dean & Son Limited © Darrell Waters Ltd, 1939, and Enid Blyton, 1946; Alice Hoffman, *Practical Magic* © 1995 Alice Hoffman, published by G. P. Putnam's Sons, New York, and General Publishing Co. Ltd, Toronto; K. E. Sullivan reprinted courtesy of The Foundry Creative Media Company; W. B. Yeats, from *The Stolen Child,* reprinted courtesy of A. P. Watt Ltd, on behalf of Anne and Michael Yeats, and taken from *The Collected Poems of W. B. Yeats;* J. R. R. Tolkien, reprinted courtesy of Unwin Hyman, a division of HarperCollins Publishers Limited, London and New York.